THE
AMAZING
ANIMAL
ALPHABET
BOOK

The AMAZING ANIMAL ALPHABET BOOK

BY ROGER AND MARIKO CHOUINARD
ILLUSTRATED BY ROGER CHOUINARD

Doubleday & Company, Inc., Garden City, New York

To the memory of my grandmother, Rosa Miller

R.C.

Library of Congress Cataloging-in-Publication Data:

Chouinard, Roger.
  The amazing animal alphabet book.

  Summary: Animals in alliterative phrases introduce the letters of the alphabet.
Examples: Kangaroos kissing in kayaks.
  1. English language—Alphabet—Juvenile literature.   2. Animals—Juvenile literature.
3. Alphabet.   4. Animals.   I. Chouinard, Mariko.   II. Title.
PE1155.C48 1988   [E]   87-13692
ISBN 0-385-24029-5   ISBN 0-385-24030-9 (lib. bdg.)

THE AMAZING ANIMAL ALPHABET BOOK

Aa

Anteater anticipating August

Bb

Bear bathing in a bathtub

Cc

Cat catching a cab

Dd

Dog and a duck dancing divinely

Ee

Elephant and an emu eating elegantly

Ff

Frog feeling forlorn

Gg

Gorilla getting into a girdle

Hh

Hippo hiding behind a hill

Ii

Iguana indulging in ice cream

Jj

Jackrabbit jumping into a jacuzzi

Kk

Kangaroos kissing in kayaks

Lions and a lamb in a lifeboat

Mm

Mole making a molehill out of a mountain

Nn

Nuthatch nibbling nuts nightly

Oo

Orangutan ogling an overweight ostrich

Pp

Parrot on a pirate parading with pigs and penguins

Qq

Quail quarreling with the queen

Rhinoceros riding in a rocketship

Ss

Stork stepping out with a snake

Tiger tailoring a tuxedo for a turkey

Uu

Unicorn in uniform on a unicycle

Vv

Vulture vacationing with his valentine

Ww

Weasel with a wig in a windstorm

Xx

X-ray fish on the xylophone at Xmas

Yy

Yak on a yacht with his yoyo

Zebra with zippers on his zoot suit

About the Author and Illustrator

ROGER CHOUINARD grew up learning his ABCs in southern California, where he attended Chouinard Art Institute before pursuing a career as an illustrator and animation director.

His wife, MARIKO, born in Tokyo, learned her ABCs in Japan before moving to the United States with her family. She graduated from the University of Southern California.

The two now have their ABCs under one roof, living in Los Angeles and helping each other produce animated television commercials. *The Amazing Animal Alphabet Book* is their first book.